©All Rights Reserved; 2016 Copyright of yanuka - books that love children.
You may not reproduce, copy, record, translate, maintain a database or transmit in any form or by any means electronic or mechanical or otherwise - any part of this book. Commercial use of this book in any form is strictly prohibited without express written permission from the publisher.

Printed in Israel in 2016

Adapted and Edited by Atara Ofek
Graphic Design by Orly Shmuel
Translation by Leonie Barel
Edit translation Helene Hart
Print producer: Haim belfer

ISBN 978-1986835442

Janusz Korczak:

The Man who Knew how to Love Children

WRITTEN AND ILLUSTRATED BY ITZCHAK BELFER

(A pupil of Janusz Korczak)

Why I Wrote This Book

Many many years ago, in the last century, I knew a very special and exceptional man, a man I will never forget. His name was Dr. Henryk Goldszmit.

Dr. Goldszmit lived in the city of Warsaw in Poland. He was a pediatrician, an educator, and a well known author who wrote his books under the pen name Janusz Korczak. Because his books were well-known, everyone got used to calling him that – Dr. Janusz Korczak. And that's what we'll call him in this story too.

So, why would I like to tell you about him? Well, that is because I was one of the few hundred orphans who were very lucky to be raised by this wonderful man. He loved children and understood them as no one else had ever understood them before, and soon there will be no one left in this world who knew him when they were children. I think it is very important that you too, the kids of today, know who Janusz Korczak was, and why any child who was fortunate enough to have known him, will never ever forget him.

Dr. Korczak, who was Jewish, wrote many books about the hardships children experienced, especially Jewish orphans. He dreamed of building a home for orphans – and this dream came true thanks to the Jewish organization Help for Orphans, which raised money through public donations to build a new orphanage for Jewish children.

It was just over a hundred years ago, in 1912, that eighty-five kids moved into their new home led by Dr. Janusz Korczak, with Miss Stefa Wilczynska at his side – as head educator. It was a beautiful, large house with four stories. There wasn't another house like it in all of Poland! That is where the doctor's dream began to take shape: creating a new world for these young residents, many of whom were orphans who had lost both their father and their mother.

I too grew up in that home, and it gave me what no other school in the world could have given a child like me. I arrived as a seven-year-old boy, and left at fifteen – practically a young man. I am now going to tell you about this wonderful and interesting period in my life.

And This Is How the Story Begins.....

My father died when I was four years old. We were six children at home, and it was very hard for my mother Esther to provide for us on her own. We moved into a much smaller apartment, with only one room, and we tried to manage somehow.

One summer morning, without any explanation or preparation, my mother helped me get dressed in my very best clothes. She then covered her head with a scarf and said to me: "Come Itzchak'ele, we're going to see a house!" I had no idea that my mother was taking me to an orphanage. She probably didn't want to scare me, so she told me nothing. Later I learned that she had been thinking about this for a very long time, till she finally decided to take me to Janusz Korczak's orphanage so that I would have a chance to grow up to be "a decent man".

Not just anyone was accepted to Korczak's orphanage – it was only for children between the ages of seven and fourteen who had lost their father or mother, and only one child from a family. The house was very famous and there were a lot of children waiting to be accepted there.

I was already seven. I went with my mother to the orphanage and we met Doctor Korczak in a large hall. The doctor led us to a tiny room at the end of the hall, where there were two chairs and a small table. He invited my mother to sit down and then he sat down beside her. There was nowhere left for me to sit, so the doctor sat me down on his lap and started talking to mother.

At first I wasn't very comfortable and I was afraid I might fall, so I hugged the doctor and began to examine him, looking at him closely. What a nice little beard he had! I was very curious and I wanted to know if his beard was real, so I touched it.

He didn't react, so I started exploring the special glasses that sat on his nose – they were small and so delicate! I pressed my cheek against his to try to see my mother through the lenses of his glasses, but I couldn't really, because that was exactly when they finished their talk.

Mother got up, and the doctor did too. He put me back down, but he didn't let go of my hand. Mother turned to me and said:

"Itzchak'ele, you will be staying here and I am going home."

I didn't even cry. I liked the man. I parted from my mother with a kiss… And that's how I got to stay at the orphanage.

The doctor turned to me. "Itzchak'ele", he said, "behind that door an older boy is waiting for you. He will be your mentor. He'll explain everything there is to know about life in this house. He'll protect you and be responsible for everything you do for the next four months. His name is Yossi."

I looked at the boy who was about thirteen. He was tall and nice, but a little serious.

My mentor led me to the showers, for my first shower at the orphanage. I was given new clothes, and it felt really good walking hand in hand with Yossi as he showed me around the entire house.

We went up to the first floor to a large hall that was divided in two: One section had tables for meals and for games. The other half was used as a play area and for performances.

At one end of this area was a small stage, and on it was a black grand piano, which a number of children were playing. At the opposite end of the hall was a large cabinet that took up the whole wall. The top part was used as a library, and the bottom was divided into 107 drawers. Each child had their own personal drawer (the older children had cubicles). There, in our drawers, we kept all of our little treasures.

"No one but you has the right to open your drawer" Yossi told me.

Suddenly a gong sounded throughout the house. "It's a signal for lunch," Yossi said.

Kids came from everywhere, none of them rushing. They washed their hands and sat down at their usual places at the tables. The older children had laid the tables beforehand, and now they were the ones serving the food. They also cleared the tables after the meal.

Yossi explained to me that all the children in the house had various chores to do during the day. Every three months you could change your chore duties.

After we finished eating, we had a little free time to play, and to do homework and all the chores that we hadn't finished during the morning, such as cleaning the stairs, the showers and all the rest.

With Yossi's help, I began to get to know the house and the children. Some of the things that amazed me most were how tidy and clean the whole house was, how quietly the children behaved, and how confident they were. Even during playtime there wasn't much shouting or fighting. Everything was done with respect and consideration.

Sometimes, despite the usual calm, we would fight each other – just like kids anywhere – and that too was organized by house rules and agreements.

The Young Judges

We had a special list for fights, which was pinned to the notice board. Whenever someone wanted to hit a friend, they would write their names down, who they wanted to fight, and when. If fights broke out suddenly, without planning, we would add ourselves to the list when the fight was over.

The notice board was really important to us. It was where our duty roster, our daily routines and special announcements were posted. That's where we made our requests, and our apologies.

The house was run by an independent student council, which we elected every year. The council decided what chores to give the new kids, it gave out merit certificates and determined all the house rules and routines…Even Korczak would submit his suggestions for changes or new rules, in writing, to the student council.

If anyone did anything to hurt anyone else, the incident would be brought before the house court. Yes, we had our very own court in the orphanage and we ourselves were the judges.

Every Saturday morning, after breakfast, the court convened with a panel of five judges, all of them kids. The judges were chosen by lottery from amongst those kids who nobody had complained about that week. The judges would sit and discuss the various complaints, read all the testimonies, and finally decide on the verdicts.

The judges' verdicts were announced at the general assembly, right after the court's session. Whatever the judges decided, was binding for every single person who lived in the house. There were no exceptions.

Once, one of the girls even filed a suit against Korczak himself! This is what happened:

The girl was hanging onto Korczak's housecoat, and she wouldn't let go of him. He could neither move nor work. He asked her several times to let him go, but nothing helped. Finally the doctor lifted her up and sat her on a high shelf.

The little girl started crying because she was afraid and she begged him, "Doctor Sir, please take me down!"

But the doctor refused. Then, one of the girl's friends called out loudly:

"Bring him to trial!"

And that is how it happened that Korczak was brought before our court.

The verdict the doctor received for this incident was called Article 100 on the list of verdicts. Article 100 states:

"What you did was wrong! The court requests that you do not do it again."

When the court judges read the doctor's verdict, we all burst out laughing. For weeks after that we jokingly called the doctor "One Hundred".

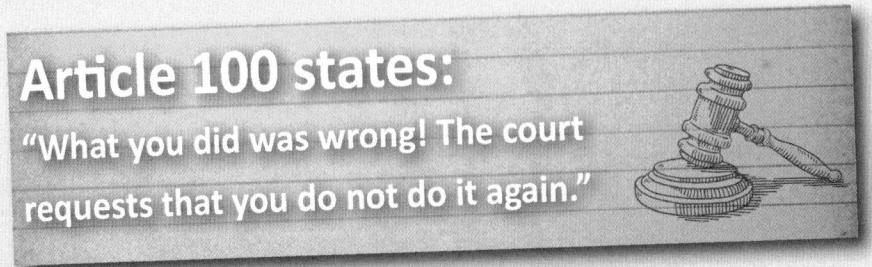

Once, Korczak even brought himself to trial. We were all astonished. We asked, "But Doctor, none of the children complained about you! Why do you want to be put on trial?"

And Korczak explained to us:

"If you do something wrong and no one witnesses it, it doesn't mean you are not responsible for your actions."

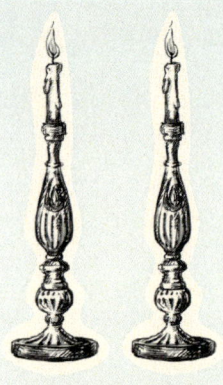

Indoors and Out

There were children at the orphanage with no family at all, and there were those like me who had a parent or other family members they could visit in Warsaw. Those of us who had family would visit them every Saturday, from noon till evening. At six in the evening we had to go back to the orphanage.

The mentors would take the younger children to visit their families on Saturdays – either on foot or by tram. My mother's home was far away, and I used to visit her by tram every Saturday, at first with Yossi, and then when I was older, on my own. I loved visiting my mother and brothers and sisters, but in the evening I was just as happy to go back "home" to Korczak, Stefa and my friends.

We attended the Jewish school, which was walking distance from the house. There we studied and spoke only in Polish. We studied Hebrew at the orphanage as an after school activity, just like the other extra activities we had.

In the morning, before we left for school, Stefa would stand at the door with two huge baskets of sandwiches. Each child would get one, two or three sandwiches, depending on how hungry they were that morning. I was one of the hungry ones, and Stefa always gave me at least two sandwiches along with a loving smile. There was a good choice of sandwiches; there was yellow cheese or white, egg or butter, and they were all delicious.

Kids came to the school from all kinds of places, and we, "Korczak's children," stood out thanks to our good manners and our quiet self-confidence. We also did well in our studies compared to everyone else.

Do you want to know why?

There was a huge library at the orphanage. Once a week, one of the older children would exchange books for the rest of us, and most of us loved reading. We read masterpieces by famous writers such as Charles Dickens, Maxim Gorky, Lev Tolstoy and Jack London, as well as books about current affairs and world events. That's how we had so much great general knowledge, over and above what we learned at school.

Sometimes in the street, on the way to or from school, Polish kids would wait to taunt us. This usually happened on Sundays when the non-Jewish children didn't have school, and we did. Sometimes there'd be real blows. When that happened we would, of course, complain to Korczak, and he would comfort us and deal with the issue in various different ways.

First Rank = Member

Second Rank = Resident

Third Rank = Resident Who Doesn't Care

There were three levels of residency at the orphanage. The highest rank was that of a member, and it was, of course, the most sought after. The next one was that of resident, and the lowest level of all was called a resident who doesn't care. I used to be something of a know-it-all and a little arrogant, so not everyone liked me. When the kids voted on our status, they always denied my request for the desirable rank of member. For years I was stuck at second rank, and it made me both angry and sad.

When I turned eleven, I went to Korczak and said:

"Doctor, I am sick of it. I have been a resident for four years. I want to be a member!"

"And why are you just a resident?" The doctor asked me.

"I know why they don't like me," I admitted, "I like to show off, because I'm excellent at sports, a good student and I know a lot of things...And I also get into a lot of fights."

"How many times a week do you fight?" asked the doctor.
I looked down, embarrassed and replied: "Every day."

"Let's make a bet," said Korczak, "that during the coming week you try to show off only three times, and fight only once. I say you won't succeed, but if you do – I'll give you a candy".

A week later the doctor asked me: "How did it go?"

I had to admit that I'd lost the bet...but I did start paying attention to my behavior and actions. The doctor would bet with other kids too, to help whoever wanted to change their ways or get rid of bad habits. The bets were very organized. They took place once a week. Anyone who wanted to bet with the doctor would get a candy for even trying, and whoever won the bet, would get another one.

That entire year I kept on betting the doctor. Every time I won the bet, I got two candies and the doctor's compliments. When I didn't, I got only one candy as compensation, and then we'd immediately bet again. In the end, I did manage to improve. I won the bets and I was made a member.

The day I rose to membership was a great day for me, and I strutted around like a peacock.

I felt like I'd really achieved something in my life.

Stefa, the head educator and house mother, was as important to the kids as Korczak himself – she took care of all our needs, and was a kind of substitute for the mothers we missed so much.

I loved making decorations for the various events and I would always sketch in my notebooks. Stefa noticed my love of drawing and recognized my special talent. When I turned nine she came to me with a serious look on her face and said:

"Itzchak'ele, I know you love drawing. I am going to give you paper, brushes and colored crayons – and in your free time you can draw in the little room."

Suddenly I had a place of my own to be alone, to daydream and to draw

The little room was where my mother and I had first met the doctor. We called it "the Store" because it was where Stefa kept the stationery she gave out to the kids. Her generous offer gave me extraordinary pleasure: Suddenly I had a place to be alone, to daydream and draw. For years I enjoyed this special privilege, and I would take the key and go into the room to draw. Neither the doctor nor Stefa ever asked to see what I had drawn, and that made me confident enough to draw whatever I felt like.

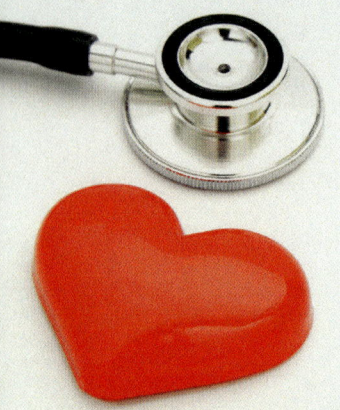

Our Doctor

To us, Korczak was very affectionate and warm. We all felt like he was one of us, and he was very easy to approach. With adults he was more distant and restrained. He was always treated with respect, as his name had become a legend throughout Poland. The story goes that he would charge a high fee when he went on calls to wealthy sick patients, but he never took any payment from the poor, and he would even leave them money to buy medicine. He and Stefa were not paid to work at the orphanage and they never asked to be paid.

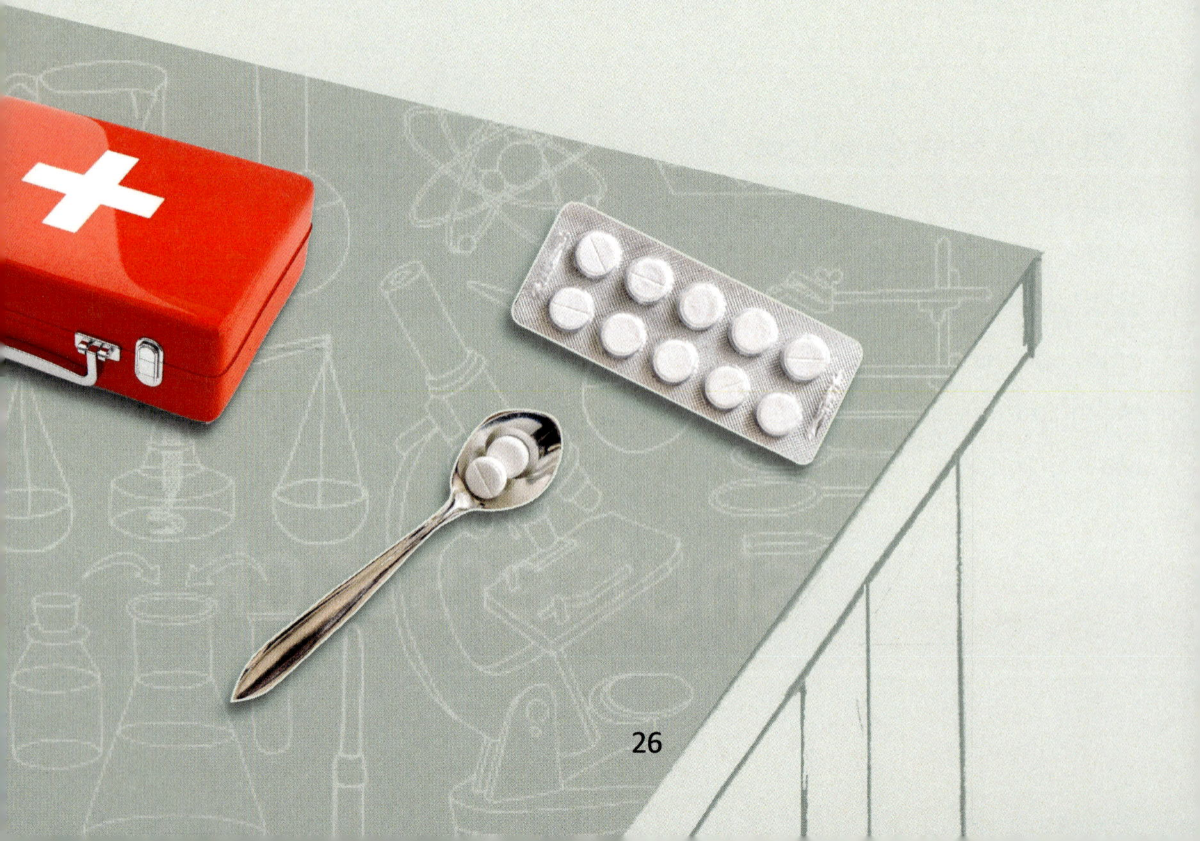

Summer Camp

In the summer, after the school year ended, we went to summer camp for two months on a huge farm that sprawled over an enormous area. We called it "our own private farm." We spent our time playing games and going on hikes in the nearby woods and dunes. Sometimes we even went as far as Vistula, the big river.

After the cramped city life in Warsaw, our vacation in nature was magical. We ran around the farmyard in short pants and barefoot. There were some chores to do on the farm, but they were easy and there weren't too many of them, things like picking up papers and cleaning the dirt off the pathway.

At camp we had our own special Olympic Games, and the group that organized it was called the Group for Beneficial Games. For three weeks they held a variety of different competitions in all kinds of sports, some of which we invented ourselves: the 100-meter dash, the 400-meter race, the high jump, the egg and spoon race, the sack race, volleyball and so many others. After every competition the results were announced to all the kids – and it was a huge honor to be one of the winners!

When the vacation was over we went home, where Stefa met us at the door with a broad smile and true amazement: "How tanned you are! Look how much you've grown!"

This is how we lived, 107 kids, in an independent children's realm. In our realm, adults had the same rights as children, or vice versa, if you wish. There was no realm like it, anywhere in the world, but I hope there will be sometime.

The house we lived in was full of love, consideration of our needs and understanding. Miss Stefa and Doctor Korczak managed to create a new, safe and just world for children, based on Janusz Korczak's wise educational approach.

And if any of you doubt or don't believe that it's possible, I suggest you read a few of the beautiful children's books that Janusz Korczak wrote, such as King Matt the First. I also really recommend two very important books for your parents to read, that Korczak wrote for adults: Loving Every Child and The Child's Right to Respect.

When I turned 14

And What Happened Later…

When I turned fourteen, I was supposed to leave the orphanage.

Naturally I didn't want to go: My mother's small home was very crowded, and besides, I was deeply attached to the orphanage – to Stefa, the doctor and all my friends.

Stefa knew that I didn't really have anywhere to go back to, and she persuaded me to write a letter to the children's council asking them to allow me to spend another year at the orphanage. I submitted the request, and luckily they allowed me to stay in that Garden of Eden for another year, till I turned fifteen.

When I turned fifteen

At fifteen I had no choice, and with great sorrow I had to leave the orphanage and go back to live with my family. Still, I visited the doctor and Stefa every Saturday. From four o'clock in the afternoon until six thirty in the evening, Korczak and Stefa would sit and talk to us, the graduates, and it was a wonderful reunion. I so loved those Saturdays.

When I was 16 the war broke out

By the time I had turned sixteen, the atmosphere in Warsaw had become very anti-Semitic and unbearably menacing. My friend from the orphanage, whose name was also Itzchak, and I, decided to escape to Russia to try to save our lives. Of course we first went to say goodbye to the home that we loved so, and to the people who had been like a father and mother to us – Korczak and Stefa. The parting was sad and difficult.

I remember Korczak quietly mumbling, "The chicks are leaving the nest…"

He asked us some questions, took some money from his pocket and gave it to us both, like a kind father. It was the last time I ever saw him, Stefa and the orphans.

Korczak didn't try to persuade us to stay in Poland. He must have known what was about to happen… two years after that, he was taken to the ghetto.

Dr. Korczak and Miss Stefa dreamed of immigrating to Israel. They had both visited a few times, but they didn't realize their dream in time. When the war broke out, they chose to stay with their little orphans in Poland. Eventually, they died with them in the death camp in Treblinka.

The older children and I remembered their stories about Israel. Thanks to these stories, we decided to immigrate to Israel, and as you can see, we succeeded, a few of my friends and I.

I am now passing the story of this wonderful man on to you, before there is no one left to remember and share his story.

Made in the USA
Monee, IL
03 October 2020

43891832R00024